Pebble® Plus

WOW!

# THE WORLD'S TALLEST HOUSE OF CARDS

## and Other Number Records

by Thomas K. and Heather Adamson

**Consulting Editor:** Gail Saunders-Smith, PhD

**CAPSTONE PRESS**
a capstone imprint

Pebble Plus is published by Capstone Press,
1710 Roe Crest Drive, North Mankato, Minnesota 56003
www.capstonepub.com

**Library of Congress Cataloging-in-Publication Data**
Adamson, Thomas K., 1970–
  The world's tallest house of cards and other number records / by Thomas K. and Heather Adamson.
     p. cm.—(Pebble Plus. Wow!)
  Audience: 6-8.
  Audience: K to grade 3.
  Summary: "Simple text and colorful photos present record-breaking facts featuring numbers"—Provided by publisher.
  Includes bibliographical references and index.
  ISBN 978-1-4765-0240-3 (library binding)—ISBN 978-1-4765-3472-5 (ebook pdf)
  1. World records—Juvenile literature. 2. Curiosities and wonders—Juvenile literature. I. Adamson, Heather, 1974– II. Title.
  AG243.A33 2014
  031.02—dc23                                                                    2013001986

**Editorial Credits**
Erika L. Shores, editor; Lori Bye, designer; Eric Gohl and Svetlana Zhurkin, media researcher;
Jennifer Walker, production specialist

**Photo Credits**
AP Photo: dapd/Mario Vedder, 13, Invision/Mattel/Max Simbron, 19, Kin Cheung, 11, Rex Features/Ray Tang, 21, *The Canadian Press*/Frank Gunn, 17; Corbis: Louie Psihoyos, 7; Newscom: WENN/PN2, 9, WENN/ZOB/CB2, 5; Shutterstock: Anneka, cover, Redshinestudio (grunge border), throughout; *The Times*, Ottawa, Illinois: Tom Sistak, 15

## Note to Parents and Teachers

The Wow! set supports national mathematics standards related to measurement. This book describes and illustrates record-breaking facts featuring numbers. The images support early readers in understanding the text. The repetition of words and phrases helps early readers learn new words. This book also introduces early readers to subject-specific vocabulary words, which are defined in the Glossary section. Early readers may need assistance to read some words and to use the Table of Contents, Glossary, Read More, Internet Sites, and Index sections of the book.

Printed in the United States of America in North Mankato, Minnesota.
032013     007223CGF13F

# TABLE OF CONTENTS

# FABULOUS FOOD RECORDS

Tallest, heaviest, fastest, strongest.

The world is full of records.

The heaviest onion weighed

18 pounds, 1 ounce (8.2 kilograms).

That's heavier than a bowling ball.

The biggest cookie ever made couldn't fit on a basketball court. Most cookie recipes need two eggs. This cookie used 30,000 eggs.

The world's biggest cookie was 102 feet (31 meters) wide.

How many hot dogs can you eat?

Joey Chestnut ate 68 hot dogs

in 10 minutes. Pass the ketchup!

Joey Chestnut

# AMAZING BUILDING RECORDS

Some records take a steady hand. And a lot of patience. The tallest house of cards was 26 feet (7.9 meters) tall. Bryan Berg used 1,100 decks of cards.

Want to set a world record for

toppling dominoes? You'll need

thousands of dominoes!

This pyramid fell in 10 seconds.

It had 13,486 dominoes.

The tallest Lincoln Log structure reached 10 feet, 11 inches (3.3 m). That's almost 1 foot (0.3 m) taller than a basketball hoop.

# MORE AMAZING RECORDS

We can measure all kinds

of records. Kevin Fast set a record

by pulling the heaviest airplane.

The airplane weighed

more than 27 elephants.

This airplane weighed 416,299 pounds (189 metric tons).

Two drivers share the record
for driving the largest loop.
The 60-foot- (18.3-m-) tall loop
was like a toy car track come
to life.

Usually only two people easily fit in a mini car. In London, England, 28 women set a record by squeezing into a Mini Cooper.

# GLOSSARY

**deck**—a pack of 52 playing cards

**measure**—to find out the size or weight of something

**patience**—the ability to put up with problems and delays without getting upset

**recipe**—directions for preparing food

**record**—when something is done better than anyone has ever done it before

**steady**—firm; not shaking or moving

**structure**—something that has been built

**topple**—to fall over slowly

# READ MORE

Aboff, Marcie, and Trisha Speed Shaskan. *Math Fun.* Minneapolis: Picture Window Books, 2010.

*Awesome Feats. Ripley's Believe It or Not!* Philadelphia: Mason Crest, 2012.

Hirschmann, Kris, and Ryan Herndon. *Guinness World Records: Ultimate Gross Records.* New York: Scholastic, 2011.

# INTERNET SITES

FactHound offers a safe, fun way to find Internet sites related to this book. All of the sites on FactHound have been researched by our staff.

Here's all you do:

Visit *www.facthound.com*

Type in this code: 9781476502403

Super-cool stuff!

Check out projects, games and lots more at
**www.capstonekids.com**

# INDEX

Word Count: 214

Grade: 1

Early-Intervention Level: 18